The Case for Philosophy in Higher Education

A Guide for Building Purpose, Skills, and Resilience in College and Beyond

I0152392

L. R. Caldwell
Author of *Consciousness: Beyond the Planck Boundary* and *The IF Trilogy: A Unified Theory of God, Mind, and Matter* Reason and Reality Publishing, 2025

The Case for Philosophy in Higher Education

© 2025 L. R. Caldwell

ISBN: 979-8-9992710-2-0
ORCID : 0009-0005-6487-9274

Published by Reason and Reality Publishing
Printed in the United States of America
Also by L. R. Caldwell:
Consciousness: Beyond the Planck Boundary
*The IF Trilogy: A Unified Theory of God, Mind, and Matter

Dedication

This book is dedicated to my uncle,
Glen M. Caldwell, ret.- Master Chief USN
and in memory of his wife,
Margie L. (Valder) Caldwell (5/1945 – 7/2011)

Beloved Wife, Mother, and Grandmother.

Contents

CHAPTER 1 — PHILOSOPHY AS CONCEPTUAL FOUNDATIONS....1

The Discipline That Grounds All Knowledge 1

Logic and the Architecture of Reasoning...1

Epistemology and the Nature of Knowledge 2

Philosophy of Mind and the Limits of AI...2

Why Conceptual Foundations Matter Today 2

Career Outcomes & Labor-Market Myths: What the Data Actually
Shows...5

Expanded Opportunities Through Continued Study.....................................5

Common Critiques of Philosophy as a Career — and Rebuttals.................6

CHAPTER 2 — PHILOSOPHY AS ETHICS AND GOVERNANCE........9

Beyond Capability: The Question of "Should"...9

Ethical Frameworks for AI..9

Governance in Practice...10

Sector Applications..10

The Role of Philosophy in Regulation 10

Historical Precedents for Governance 11

Global Perspectives on AI Ethics..11

Case Study: Facial Recognition in Policing...11

Corporate Responsibility and Ethical Cultures 12

Future Challenges in Governance..12

Philosophy as a Safeguard Against Technocratic Drift..............................12

Notes for Chapter 2..13

CHAPTER 3 — PHILOSOPHY AS INTERDISCIPLINARY PROBLEM SOLVING..15

Philosophy as Problem Clarifier..15

Translating Across Disciplines..15

Building Trust Through Clarity..16

Illustrative Dialogue..17

Interdisciplinary Research Teams..17

Climate and Environmental Policy..18

The Bridge to Practice..18

CHAPTER 4 — THE UPSKILLING PATH FOR PHILOSOPHY MAJORS..21

Introduction: Philosophy as Foundation, Not Limitation..21

Section 1: The Logic-to-Technology Bridge..21

Section 2: Epistemology and Knowledge Systems..22

Section 3: Ethics as a Professional Compass..23

Section 4: Philosophy of Mind and Cognitive Science..23

Section 5: Philosophy and Law..24

Section 6: Business, Economics, and Leadership..24

Section 7: Philosophy and Public Policy..25

Section 8: Philosophy and Artificial Intelligence..25

Section 9: Roadmap for Students..26

Conclusion: From Foundation to Frontier..27

Critical Reasoning and Problem-Solving..27

Communication and Persuasion..28

Ethical Judgment and Integrity..28

Employment and Earnings..28

Graduate and Professional Success..28

Law and Justice...29

Medicine and Healthcare..29

Business and Leadership..29

Technology and AI..30

Public Policy and Governance...30

Addressing Common Critiques...30

Adaptability and Intellectual Humility...................................31

Conclusion: A Foundation That Endures................................31

CHAPTER 5 — CAREER PATHWAYS AND PROFESSIONAL
OUTCOMES..33

Introduction: From Training to Trajectory.............................33

Critical Reasoning and Problem-Solving................................33

Communication and Persuasion...33

Ethical Judgment and Integrity..33

Employment and Earnings..34

Graduate and Professional Success...34

Addressing Common Critiques...35

Adaptability and Intellectual Humility...................................35

Beyond Employment: Philosophy and Purpose.....................35

Conclusion: Outcomes That Endure..36

CHAPTER 6 — FROM CLASSROOM TO IMPACT: A PHILOSOPHY
PLAYBOOK FOR REAL-WORLD RESULTS..............................37

Research and Data Literacy (Without the Pitfalls)................38

Communicating Across Disciplines...38

Ethics as Design, Not showmanship.......................................39

A Semester-by-Semester Roadmap...39

First Semester..39

Second Semester...40

Third Semester..40

Fourth Semester..40

Fifth Semester...40

Sixth Semester..41

Seventh Semester..41

Eighth Semester..41

Programmatic Recommendations for Departments...............41

Simplified Summary..42

Notes...43

CHAPTER 7 — PHILOSOPHY AS MEANING AND PURPOSE............45

1) The Limits of Machines on "Why"................................45

2) Purpose Before Performance..46

3) Identity in an Age of Technology..................................47

4) Wisdom Versus Intelligence..48

5) Education for Meaning..49

8) Conclusion: Meaning as Humanity's Safeguard 51

Simplified Summary..51

References..52

CHAPTER 8 — PHILOSOPHY AS SOCIETY'S COMPASS...................53

Philosophy as Cultural Foundation...................................53

The Compass in Governance..54

Guiding Science and Technology......................................54

Philosophy as a Unifying Language...................................55

The Ethical Compass in Crisis...56

Education for Civic Responsibility....................................56

CHAPTER 9 — PHILOSOPHY AS PREPARATION FOR LIFE............59

1) Orientation: Why "Preparation for Life" Is Philosophical...................59

2) Decision-Making Under Uncertainty 59

3) Resilience and Character...60

4) Communication and Persuasion..61

5) Ethical Living: From Values to Design...61

6) Financial Reasoning for Philosophers..62

7) Civic Literacy and Public Reason...62

Conclusion: A Coherent Life...64

Simplified Summary..64

CHAPTER 10— PHILOSOPHY AS GUIDANCE FOR PARENTS AND COUNSELORS...67

A Pathway for Parents Themselves..68

Small Starts for Parents...68

Shared Language at Home..69

Philosophy as a Bridge Across Generations.......................................69

Understanding the Generational Gap...69

Reasoning Toward Harmony 70

Simplified Summary..70

Suggested Reading for Parents and Counselors..................................71

Chapter 11: Philosophers Who Shaped the Understanding of Mind and Reality...73

Gottfried Wilhelm Leibniz 73

René Descartes...74

Immanuel Kant...74

Aristotle...75

John Locke..75

Martin Heidegger...76

Gilbert Ryle...76

John Searle...77

Martha Nussbaum...77

Bibliography...78

Appendix of Study and Discussion Questions............................81

Chapter 1 — Philosophy as Conceptual Foundations..............81

Chapter 2 — Philosophy as Ethics and Governance...............81

Chapter 3 — Philosophy as Interdisciplinary Problem Solving..............81

Chapter 4 — The Upskilling Path for Philosophy Majors..........82

Chapter 5 — Career Pathways and Professional Outcomes.....82

Chapter 6 — From Classroom to Impact: A Philosophy Playbook for Real-World Results...82

Chapter 7 — Philosophy as Meaning and Purpose..................83

Chapter 8 — Philosophy as Society's Compass.......................83

Chapter 9 — Philosophy as Preparation for Life......................83

Chapter 10 — Philosophy as Guidance for Parents and Counselors......84

For Parents...84

For Counselors...84

About the Author..85

CHAPTER 1 — PHILOSOPHY AS CONCEPTUAL FOUNDATIONS

Philosophy has always served as the discipline that undergirds all structured human knowledge. From the earliest records of human inquiry, philosophy provided the conceptual scaffolding that allowed law, science, and mathematics to take root. What we now call "fields" or "disciplines" were originally branches of philosophy, unified by a search for coherent principles that explain how reality operates and how reasoning can guide human life.

The Discipline That Grounds All Knowledge

Philosophy is not an isolated practice but the foundation for every other intellectual pursuit. Aristotle's syllogisms gave structure to rational argument; Leibniz's dream of a universal calculus anticipated formal logic and computation; Kant's critical philosophy set conditions for how human understanding interprets reality. Without philosophy, concepts like evidence, justice, or scientific method would lack coherence. Law depends on philosophy to define fairness, while science depends on epistemology to clarify what counts as knowledge.

Logic and the Architecture of Reasoning

Logic, the oldest branch of philosophy, remains central today. Aristotle formalized syllogistic reasoning, creating patterns that shaped centuries of thought. Centuries later, Gottlob Frege and Bertrand Russell transformed logic into symbolic systems capable of expressing mathematical proofs. Alan Turing, drawing on this tradition, showed the boundaries of computation itself, laying the foundation of computer science. Every line of code written today is a descendant of these philosophical insights. Likewise, medical ethics frameworks, legal reasoning, and economic fairness debates are also rooted in philosophical traditions, showing that philosophy's influence extends far beyond the digital realm.

Epistemology and the Nature of Knowledge

Epistemology asks: what does it mean to "know"? How do we distinguish justified belief from mere opinion? These questions are no less urgent in the age of Artificial Intelligence. When an AI system recommends a diagnosis, or a financial decision, is it truly "knowledge" or only statistical inference? Philosophical clarity is indispensable in evaluating what we can and cannot trust from our machines—and just as crucial in medicine, law, and governance, where the same principles guide decisions about justice, fairness, and human dignity.

Philosophy of Mind and the Limits of AI

The philosophy of mind considers questions of consciousness, cognition, and representation. Can machines understand, or are they only simulating understanding? This distinction is not trivial. Mistaking sophisticated pattern recognition for genuine awareness risks confusing mechanical efficiency with human depth. Philosophy reminds us that intelligence without consciousness is not the same as human reasoning—and that conflating the two can mislead both engineers and society.

Why Conceptual Foundations Matter Today

Philosophy ensures that our technological progress remains coherent, ethical, and intelligible. Without conceptual grounding, systems risk being powerful yet incoherent, effective yet unaccountable. Philosophy continues to provide the conceptual framework by which we navigate science, law, and engineering—ensuring that intelligence, human or artificial, is anchored in clarity and responsibility.

It is easy to assume that only coders and engineers contribute to AI, but philosophy has shaped the field from the beginning. From the early logic of computation to today's debates about alignment, interpretability, and agency, philosophical questions are embedded in AI's core.

Philosophers influence conceptual design by asking: What counts as reasoning? What is intelligence? How do we know if an AI system is interpreting correctly? They contribute to interpretability research aimed at making AI decisions transparent and accountable to human reasoning standards.

Human–AI interaction is another arena where philosophy matters. How AI communicates, how it respects human values, and how it avoids manipulation are not only technical challenges—they are philosophical ones. By working alongside engineers, philosophers help ensure AI reflects coherent reasoning principles and ethical clarity, rather than becoming an opaque, unaccountable force.

Philosophy provides the foundation; targeted upskilling extends it. This is not a rejection of philosophy but an application of it—pairing philosophical reasoning with technical fluency.

The bridges are natural: logic translates into computer science fundamentals; epistemology connects to knowledge representation and reasoning (KRR); philosophy of language grounds natural language processing (NLP); and ethics ties directly into AI safety and alignment. With coursework in programming, data science, or cognitive science, philosophy majors transition smoothly into technical roles.

The combination of philosophical depth and technical skill produces thinkers who shape not just AI's capabilities but its trajectory. In the 21st century, this dual competency may become one of the most valuable skill sets.

Philosophy is not confined to classrooms or career paths—it permeates everyday life. Those trained in philosophy carry with them habits of clear thinking, careful listening, and reasoned dialogue that shape the way they interact with others.

Because philosophy cultivates abstract reasoning, graduates learn to see the hidden structures beneath ordinary conversations. Whether talking about politics, business, science, literature, or ethics, they can connect ideas across disciplines and guide discussions toward clarity rather than confusion. This ability makes them effective communicators, colleagues, and leaders in settings far beyond academia.

Philosophy also nurtures intellectual humility—the recognition that every perspective contains both insight and limitation. In personal relationships, this fosters empathy and the ability to defuse conflict by identifying the assumptions beneath disagreements. In community and civic life, it enables individuals to elevate conversations above slogans and soundbites, grounding them instead in logic, evidence, and fairness.

These qualities mean that philosophy graduates can contribute meaningfully in virtually any field, not only through professional expertise but also through the kind of conversation that builds trust, collaboration, and understanding. In a world filled with noise and division, the philosopher's voice is often the one that brings coherence.

Career Outcomes & Labor-Market Myths: What the Data Actually Shows

Contrary to popular belief, philosophy graduates do not disappear into unemployment. In fact, unemployment for philosophy majors is still considered relatively low according to recent statistics, comparable to many other large fields. Much of this strength comes from the way philosophy equips students with versatile skills—critical thinking, logical analysis, and clear communication—that enable them to excel in a wide range of careers. As a result, alumni often go on to thrive in fields such as law, policy, business, technology, and analytics.

Expanded Opportunities Through Continued Study

While earning a bachelor's degree in philosophy opens many doors, each subsequent degree magnifies the number of doors and possibilities available to philosophy graduates. Continuing your education in philosophy carries significant advantages:

• Specialization and Expertise, Advanced degrees allow students to focus deeply in areas such as logic, ethics, metaphysics, or philosophy of mind, making them subject-matter experts in fields that intersect with law, technology, and policy.

• Competitive Advantage, Graduate study enhances employability in academia, law, consulting, and public policy, where advanced analytical and ethical skills are at a premium.

• Interdisciplinary Reach, A master's or doctorate provides stronger credentials for collaboration across disciplines, particularly in AI ethics, bioethics, and cognitive science.

• Leadership Pathways, Many leadership roles in universities, think tanks, corporations, and government recruit from advanced-degree holders in philosophy because they combine broad reasoning skills with demonstrated depth.

• Lifelong Learning and Retention, Universities value philosophy majors who advance to graduate programs, as their persistence boosts retention metrics and enriches campus intellectual life.

Common Critiques of Philosophy as a Career — and Rebuttals

Critique 1: "Philosophy is impractical and does not prepare students for real-world jobs."

Rebuttal: Philosophy equips students with universal skills—critical reasoning, clarity in communication, and ethical decision-making—that apply across fields. Unlike narrow vocational training, philosophy builds adaptability. In a volatile job market, adaptability is a practical edge.

Critique 2: "Philosophy graduates struggle with unemployment and low salaries."

Rebuttal: For recent graduates, New York Fed data indicate that unemployment for philosophy majors is low by historical standards and comparable to (or lower than) many large fields in the same period. Over the longer run, humanities outcomes remain broadly similar to other majors. Salary growth often accelerates as graduates enter law, policy, business, technology, and analytics roles in which reasoning skills are at a premium.

Critique 3: "Philosophy is only for academia; it doesn't matter outside the classroom."

Rebuttal: Philosophy graduates work in law, business, technology, government, design research, and AI ethics. They are recruited to clarify goals, interrogate assumptions, and translate complexity for cross-functional teams—functions that are central to modern organizations.

Critique 4: "In the age of AI, only technical skills matter."

Rebuttal: Technical expertise without philosophical clarity risks powerful systems with no ethical philosophy. AI's most urgent challenges—bias, transparency, and alignment—are as philosophical as they are technical. Engineering teams increasingly integrate ethicists and philosophers to set standards, evaluate trade-offs, and align systems with human values.

- Weinberg, Steven. *The Quantum Theory of Fields, Volume I: Foundations*. Cambridge University Press, 1995.

- Peskin, Michael E., and Daniel V. Schroeder. *An Introduction to Quantum Field Theory*. Westview Press, 1995.

- Alan Turing, "On Computable Numbers, with an Application to the Entscheidungsproblem," *Proceedings of the London Mathematical Society*, 1936, establishing limits of computation.

- Gottlob Frege, *Begriffsschrift* (1879), introducing symbolic logic; Bertrand Russell, *Principia Mathematica* (1910–1913), expanding logical formalism.

- Immanuel Kant, *Critique of Pure Reason* (1781), for the conditions of human understanding.

- Leibniz, *Monadology* (1714) and *Discourse on Metaphysics* (1686), for the vision of a universal calculus.

- Aristotle, *Prior Analytics*, on the foundations of syllogistic logic.

CHAPTER 2 — PHILOSOPHY AS ETHICS AND GOVERNANCE

Building on the conceptual foundations of Chapter 1, we now turn from questions of what knowledge is to questions of what ought to guide action—ethics and governance. Here the focus shifts from the logic of inquiry to the responsibilities that follow from it.

As technology advances, the critical question has shifted from "What can we build?" to "What should we build?" This distinction between capability and responsibility is philosophical at its core. Philosophy equips us to evaluate not only the efficiency of systems but their legitimacy, fairness, and moral standing.

Beyond Capability: The Question of "Should"

Technical expertise enables the construction of powerful systems. But philosophy determines whether those systems are justifiable. An AI system that can predict crime, allocate healthcare resources, or screen financial applications may function flawlessly from a technical perspective yet still generate social harm. Only ethical reasoning clarifies when and how such systems should be applied.

Ethical Frameworks for AI

Three traditions in moral philosophy provide distinct approaches to evaluating AI:

- **Utilitarianism** measures outcomes by overall well-being. For AI, this perspective might guide resource allocation in healthcare or climate response, though it struggles to measure well-being across diverse populations.

- **Deontology** emphasizes duties and rights. In AI, this approach protects principles such as privacy, fairness, and respect for persons, even when utilitarian reasoning might trade them for aggregate benefit.

- **Virtue Ethics** focuses on the character of agents and the cultivation of trust. Applied to AI design, virtue ethics demands not only efficient outcomes but systems that reflect dignity, integrity, and human flourishing.

Governance in Practice

Ethics must be paired with governance structures. In the United States, the NIST AI Risk Management Framework emphasizes transparency, accountability, and trustworthiness. The European Union's AI Act requires human oversight of high-risk systems. Both initiatives rely on philosophical clarity: What does "trustworthy" mean? How do we define "fairness"?

Sector Applications

- **Justice**: Predictive policing and sentencing algorithms risk reducing justice to probability distributions. Philosophy ensures that moral responsibility is not overshadowed by statistics.

- **Finance**: Automated credit and insurance models may encode discrimination. Ethical reasoning exposes hidden biases and insists on human accountability. This is as true in environmental policy and climate governance as it is in AI, where competing priorities must be balanced by coherent values.

- **Healthcare**: Diagnostic AI can reinforce inequities if trained on biased datasets. Philosophical frameworks demand patient dignity and fairness remain central.

The Role of Philosophy in Regulation

Policymakers require more than technical compliance checklists; they require conceptual clarity. Philosophers ensure regulation reflects democratic values and human dignity rather than market expediency. In this way, philosophy becomes not only a critic of technology but an active partner in governance.

Historical Precedents for Governance

Philosophical reflection on governance is not new. Plato's Republic explored the dangers of unchecked power, while Aristotle emphasized the importance of virtue in political life. These ancient concerns mirror today's debates about AI governance: how to balance efficiency with justice, and how to ensure that systems of power remain accountable to the people they serve. The continuity of these questions demonstrates that while technology evolves, the ethical dilemmas it raises are deeply human and enduring.

Global Perspectives on AI Ethics

Governance challenges also vary across cultures. The United States often emphasizes innovation and market flexibility, relying on frameworks such as the NIST AI Risk Management Framework. The European Union emphasizes human rights and risk-based regulation through the AI Act. Meanwhile, countries in Asia, including Japan and South Korea, highlight AI's role in social harmony and collective good. These differences reveal how cultural values shape the ethical priorities of governance, and why philosophy is essential in navigating a truly global landscape of AI oversight.

Case Study: Facial Recognition in Policing

Consider the debate around facial recognition technologies. From a technical standpoint, these systems may achieve high accuracy rates. Yet their deployment raises questions of privacy, surveillance, and potential bias. Utilitarian reasoning may defend the technology as a means of enhancing security, but deontological principles caution against infringing on individual rights. Virtue ethics would ask whether normalizing surveillance erodes public trust and dignity. By applying these frameworks, philosophy helps policymakers and communities evaluate not only the effectiveness but also the legitimacy of such technologies.

Corporate Responsibility and Ethical Cultures

Governance is not limited to states and regulators. Corporations play a central role in shaping AI through their design choices and deployment strategies. Philosophers can help organizations cultivate ethical cultures that prioritize fairness, accountability, and long-term responsibility over short-term profit. When companies adopt virtue-ethics frameworks—fostering integrity and trustworthiness—they move beyond compliance checklists and begin embedding ethics into the very DNA of innovation.

Future Challenges in Governance

Emerging applications such as autonomous weapons, deep fake technologies, and brain–computer interfaces raise profound ethical dilemmas. Traditional governance frameworks may not fully anticipate the risks posed by these innovations. Philosophy provides a forward-looking perspective, equipping society with the conceptual tools needed to anticipate harms before they arise. In doing so, it ensures that technological ambition remains tethered to human values and global stability.

Philosophy as a Safeguard Against Technocratic Drift

Finally, philosophy serves as a safeguard against reducing governance to technical expertise alone. While engineers and data scientists provide crucial knowledge, the ultimate questions—about justice, dignity, and the meaning of progress—cannot be settled by technical metrics. Philosophical reasoning ensures governance remains democratic, accessible, and humane, preventing societies from sliding into a technocracy where efficiency outweighs human worth.

- For U.S. concerns on neural data privacy, see: *The Verge*, "FTC Urged to Investigate Neurotech Companies," April 2025.
- For specific policy recommendations on BCIs, see: arXiv preprint, "Policy Recommendations for Next-Generation BCIs," June 2025.
- For anticipatory governance of Brain–Computer Interfaces (BCIs), see: OECD, *Brain–Computer Interfaces and the Governance System*, 2022.
- On Japan's soft-law approach in AI governance, see: Center for Strategic and International Studies (CSIS), "Norms in New Technological Domains: Japan's AI Governance Strategy," June 2025.
- Japan's AI ethics emphasizes harmony, responsibility, and long-term thinking. See: *IT Business Today*, "How Japan is Addressing Ethical Challenges in Artificial Intelligence," May 2025.

Notes for Chapter 2

With ethical frameworks and governance structures in view from Chapter 2, Chapter 3 shows philosophy at work as a practical translator across disciplines—clarifying problems, mapping trade-offs, and helping diverse experts reach coherent decisions.

CHAPTER 3 — PHILOSOPHY AS INTERDISCIPLINARY PROBLEM SOLVING

Philosophy is not confined to abstraction; it is the art of clarifying problems across disciplines. Philosophers act as intellectual translators, enabling dialogue between fields that otherwise speak different languages. In the age of complexity, this capacity is indispensable.

Philosophy as Problem Clarifier

In an era defined by accelerating specialization, the need for interdisciplinary dialogue has grown urgent. Complex problems—from pandemics to cybersecurity—rarely fit neatly within one discipline. By stepping outside disciplinary silos, philosophers provide the connective reasoning that allows experts to cooperate without reducing problems to only one dimension. This bridging role explains why universities, corporations, and governments increasingly seek out philosophy-trained voices when navigating high-stakes issues.

Complex challenges often span multiple domains—technical, ethical, social, and political. Philosophers specialize in breaking vague or contested questions into precise ones, mapping assumptions, and revealing hidden contradictions. This role allows experts from different disciplines to collaborate effectively.

Translating Across Disciplines

- **Medicine**: AI triage systems must balance patient autonomy with efficiency. Philosophers clarify the stakes, ensuring human dignity is preserved. Similar clarity is brought to bioethics, climate adaptation strategies, and economic fairness policies, where trade-offs must be mapped with precision.

Clarifying assumptions is more than an intellectual exercise; it is a safeguard against costly mistakes. A poorly framed medical trial, for example, may confuse correlation with causation, leading to wasted resources and ethical breaches. Similarly, a misinterpreted economic indicator can distort fiscal policy. Philosophers help prevent these errors by ensuring that the framing of questions is rigorous before experiments, budgets, or regulations are set into motion.

- **Law**: Contract analysis systems must interpret fairness, obligation, and intent. Philosophers guide the conceptual frameworks that shape these interpretations.

- **Education**: Adaptive learning algorithms risk embedding inequities. Philosophical clarity ensures efficiency does not eclipse justice.

Although medicine, law, and education may appear unrelated, the same philosophical skills apply across each. All three must balance efficiency against fairness, clarity against ambiguity, and individual needs against systemic goals. By exposing these structural parallels, philosophers equip specialists to learn from one another's fields rather than working in isolation. Insights gained in one sector often enrich decision-making in another, creating a more coherent approach to societal challenges.

Building Trust Through Clarity

Public trust depends not only on technical accuracy but also on transparency. Philosophers excel at communicating abstract concepts to diverse audiences, helping communities understand and evaluate the technologies that shape their lives.

One of the most overlooked contributions philosophers make is their role in countering misinformation. When the public receives conflicting or confusing reports—whether about vaccines, financial risks, or climate models—it is philosophical clarity that helps rebuild trust. By separating evidence from opinion, showing how concepts interrelate, and identifying limits of certainty, philosophers help communities regain confidence in institutions that otherwise risk losing credibility.

Illustrative Dialogue

Imagine an interdisciplinary AI project team. Engineers propose a model to allocate medical resources, prioritizing efficiency. Doctors insist on patient choice. Policymakers stress equity. The philosopher steps in—not to impose answers, but to clarify assumptions. By articulating trade-offs between efficiency, autonomy, and fairness, the philosopher enables reasoned dialogue that leads to coherent solutions. This same bridge-building role has proven essential in cross-cultural diplomacy, climate negotiations, and public health crises.

Crisis teams especially benefit from philosophical mediation. In moments where decisions must be made under intense pressure—disaster relief, national security, or pandemic response—specialists often disagree on priorities. The philosopher's task is not to dictate outcomes but to map values and risks in a way that prevents paralysis. By doing so, philosophy provides the deliberative breathing room necessary for coherent and humane responses.

Interdisciplinary Research Teams

Systems thinking also shows philosophy's enduring value. Technical models can describe feedback loops and risk thresholds, but philosophy ensures those models remain accountable to human purposes. Whether applied to ecological resilience or financial stability, philosophy prevents narrow optimization from undermining long-term coherence. By insisting on resilience as a normative principle, philosophy keeps systems oriented toward survival and justice rather than short-term efficiency alone.

Climate and Environmental Policy

For students, these interdisciplinary habits become practical advantages. Employers across law, business, healthcare, and technology value individuals who can clarify assumptions, translate between experts, and maintain coherence under complexity. Philosophy's training in these skills not only enriches intellectual life but also provides graduates with a versatile toolkit for careers. This is why philosophy is not merely an academic pursuit—it is professional preparation for navigating the real world, a natural bridge to the practical pathways outlined in the next chapter.

The Bridge to Practice

This is not an incidental skill but philosophy's natural strength. By clarifying assumptions, comparing frameworks, and fostering dialogue, philosophers ensure that advances in one field do not undermine values in another. Philosophy, in this sense, is the hidden bridge that allows society to progress coherently amidst complexity.

- For interdisciplinary AI governance frameworks: National Institute of Standards and Technology. *AI Risk Management Framework (AI RMF 1.0)*, 2023; European Union. *AI Act (Regulation (EU) 2024/1689)*.

- Historical case: Alan Turing's logical foundations and wartime codebreaking, see Hodges, Andrew. *Alan Turing: The Enigma*. Princeton University Press, 2014.

- On education and adaptive learning bias: UNESCO, *Artificial Intelligence in Education: Challenges and Opportunities*, 2021.

- On law and fairness in AI contract review: Lawrence Solum, "Artificial philosophy in Natural Law," *Journal of Legal Analysis*, 2020.

Having seen philosophy operate as an interdisciplinary bridge, the next chapter turns to practice: concrete upskilling paths that pair philosophical training with domain-specific methods and tools.

- On medical ethics in AI triage: Beauchamp, Tom L., and James F. Childress. *Principles of Biomedical Ethics*. Oxford University Press, 2019.

CHAPTER 4 — THE UPSKILLING PATH FOR PHILOSOPHY MAJORS

Introduction: Philosophy as Foundation, Not Limitation

This chapter outlines clear pathways for philosophy majors who want to extend their training into other domains—law, medicine, business, policy, technology, and yes, artificial intelligence. The message is simple: philosophy is never an endpoint; it is the launchpad for interdisciplinary mastery.

Section 1: The Logic-to-Technology Bridge

Logic is the oldest branch of philosophy, yet it also underpins modern computation. Aristotle's syllogisms, Frege's symbolic logic, and Russell's formalism culminated in Alan Turing's demonstration of computability. Today, every algorithm and program rests on this heritage.

For philosophy majors, upskilling in computer science is a natural extension. Coursework in discrete mathematics, algorithms, and programming builds directly on logical reasoning. This does not mean every philosophy major must become a software engineer. Instead, it means that their capacity for abstract reasoning translates smoothly into technical learning.

Practical roadmap:
- Introductory courses in Python and discrete mathematics.
- Specialized study in knowledge representation and reasoning (KRR) for those interested in AI.
- Exploration of formal verification and logic programming, where philosophical precision directly shapes computational reliability.

Section 2: Epistemology and Knowledge Systems

Epistemology—the study of knowledge—asks what it means to "know" something and how justified belief differs from opinion. This question lies at the heart of scientific method, legal standards of evidence, and technological systems.

Philosophy majors can upskill by studying:
- Library and information science, focusing on classification, data curation, and knowledge retrieval.
- Data science and statistics, emphasizing how data becomes evidence.
- Research methods in psychology, sociology, or medicine, where epistemology informs experimental design.

In applied settings, epistemology-trained graduates often excel in policy analysis, risk assessment, and data governance. They are equipped not only to handle numbers, but to interpret what those numbers actually mean.

Section 3: Ethics as a Professional Compass

Ethics is one of philosophy's most visible contributions to society. From business ethics to bioethics, professionals must navigate competing values. Philosophy majors who specialize in ethics are in demand across many sectors:

- Medicine and healthcare: bioethics committees, hospital review boards, public health policy.
- Law and governance: regulatory frameworks, compliance, and rights-based advocacy.
- Corporate responsibility: shaping cultures of integrity and trustworthiness.

Upskilling opportunities:
- Graduate study in bioethics or applied ethics.
- Certificate programs in regulatory compliance or public health ethics.
- Training in corporate social responsibility (CSR) and sustainability practices.

Ethics-trained philosophers often become the moral interpreters of their institutions, clarifying not just what can be done, but what should be done.

Section 4: Philosophy of Mind and Cognitive Science

Questions about consciousness, cognition, and representation belong to the philosophy of mind. In recent decades, they have merged with neuroscience, psychology, and cognitive science.

Philosophy majors can extend into:

- Cognitive psychology and experimental design.
- Neuroscience, including neuroethics and consciousness studies.
- Human-computer interaction, especially how systems communicate philosophy.

Section 5: Philosophy and Law

Upskilling pathways:
- Pre-law coursework in constitutional law, political science, and legal writing.
- Internships with policy organizations or legal advocacy groups.
- Training in jurisprudence and the philosophy of law.

Philosophy majors entering law bring a capacity for careful argumentation and ethical reflection that makes them not only competent lawyers but influential leaders in justice reform and policy.

Section 6: Business, Economics, and Leadership
Philosophy graduates often thrive in business because of their ability to clarify assumptions, negotiate philosophy, and think strategically.

Upskilling options include:
- MBA programs, where philosophy's clarity of reasoning adds value to management training.
- Specialized study in business ethics, decision theory, and strategic communication.

- Training in economic theory and behavioral economics, where assumptions about human rationality are interrogated.

Philosophy does not oppose business—it strengthens it by ensuring that profit is balanced by fairness, trust, and human dignity.

Section 7: Philosophy and Public Policy

Governance requires conceptual clarity. Policymakers face trade-offs between efficiency, justice, and democratic accountability. Philosophy majors are well-positioned to translate complex issues into coherent frameworks.

Upskilling roadmap:
- Graduate study in public policy or political philosophy.
- Training in international relations, diplomacy, or conflict resolution.
- Courses in statistics and economics to strengthen empirical analysis.

From local government to global organizations, philosophy-trained policymakers ask the questions others overlook: What is fairness? What does justice demand? How do we define progress?

Section 8: Philosophy and Artificial Intelligence

While not every philosophy major will pursue AI, the field is a powerful example of philosophy in action. AI development requires clarity about logic, knowledge, ethics, and human philosophy—all of which are philosophical domains.

Roles for philosophy-trained graduates include:
- Conceptual design: defining what counts as reasoning or knowledge in AI systems.
- Interpretability research: making machine decisions transparent.
- AI governance and ethics: ensuring that technology serves human values.
- Human–AI interaction: clarifying dialogue, trust, and responsibility.

Upskilling pathways:
- Courses in logic, algorithms, and programming.
- Training in data ethics and AI safety frameworks.
- Interdisciplinary programs in philosophy and computer science.

AI is not the only frontier for philosophy, but it illustrates vividly why philosophy is indispensable in shaping the future of technology.

Section 9: Roadmap for Students
For students asking, "What should I do next?" the following roadmap provides guidance:

1. Pair philosophy with applied courses: statistics, programming, economics, or biology.
2. Pursue internships where abstract reasoning meets practice—law firms, research labs, NGOs, or corporate ethics offices.

3. Join interdisciplinary programs: philosophy combined with neuroscience, cognitive science, or computer science.

4. Seek graduate training where philosophy intersects with applied domains (bioethics, law, policy, AI governance).

5. Maintain the philosophical core: clarity, ethics, and philosophy must guide all professional extensions.

Conclusion: From Foundation to Frontier

Philosophy majors are not limited by their degree. Instead, they hold the most versatile toolkit of reasoning and ethical clarity. With targeted upskilling, they can move into law, medicine, business, governance, or AI—fields where human responsibility is as vital as technical skill.

The lesson is clear: philosophy is not an isolated pursuit. It is the foundation of human progress. Upskilling ensures that this foundation connects with practice, shaping professionals who are not only intelligent, but wise.

Critical Reasoning and Problem-Solving

Philosophy trains students to identify assumptions, expose flaws, and construct rigorous arguments. These habits of thought directly serve legal reasoning, policy debates, business negotiations, and strategy design. Employers consistently highlight critical thinking as among the most desired competencies, and philosophy provides it at the highest level.

Communication and Persuasion

Clarity of thought produces clarity of speech and writing. Philosophy graduates are skilled in framing complex problems for varied audiences, a capacity invaluable in leadership, consulting, law, and education. In an age of fragmented communication, the philosopher's ability to articulate coherent arguments is a professional advantage.

Ethical Judgment and Integrity

Modern careers increasingly require navigating questions of fairness and responsibility. Whether in medicine, finance, or corporate governance, decisions must be evaluated for legitimacy as well as efficiency. Philosophical training ensures professionals can weigh trade-offs and defend their choices on principled grounds.

Employment and Earnings

Data counters the myth that philosophy leads to unemployment. According to the Federal Reserve Bank of New York (2025, Q2), unemployment for philosophy graduates is relatively low, comparable to many large fields. Salaries, while modest at entry, rise steadily and often surpass other humanities and social sciences by mid-career.

Graduate and Professional Success

Philosophy serves as a powerful springboard to advanced study:

- Law: Philosophy majors regularly achieve top LSAT scores due to their logical and analytical skills.
- Medicine: Training in ethics and epistemology prepares graduates for complex clinical decisions.
- Business: MBA programs recruit philosophy graduates for their communication and strategic clarity.
- Academia: Philosophy itself remains a path for teaching and research, where its questions remain vital.

The American Academy of Arts & Sciences (2021 update) confirms that philosophy majors consistently perform among the strongest on standardized graduate exams, reflecting the field's training in reasoning and abstraction.

Law and Justice
Philosophy clarifies justice, obligation, and fairness—the bedrock of law. Law schools prize philosophy graduates, and many go on to shape both legal theory and policy reform.

Medicine and Healthcare
In healthcare, philosophy equips practitioners and policymakers to weigh patient autonomy, dignity, and justice. Philosophers contribute to hospital ethics boards and public health policy, ensuring that technical decisions remain humane.

Business and Leadership
Philosophical training enhances strategic thinking and ethical oversight in business. Leaders who balance profit

with fairness and trustworthiness often rely on philosophical reasoning to guide corporate cultures.

Technology and AI
Philosophy underpins logic, knowledge, and ethics—the very foundations of artificial intelligence. Increasingly, companies hire philosophers for roles in AI governance, fairness, and interpretability, where technical expertise must be matched by conceptual clarity.

Public Policy and Governance
Governance requires more than efficiency; it requires coherent principles. Philosophers in think tanks and policy institutes articulate values of justice and fairness that shape law, diplomacy, and civic life.

Addressing Common Critiques

- "Philosophy is impractical."
Philosophy provides universal skills—reasoning, communication, ethical judgment—that transfer across sectors.

- "Philosophy graduates face unemployment."
Labor-market data shows relatively low unemployment and steady salary growth over time.

- "Only STEM matters in the AI era."
Without philosophical clarity, technology risks incoherence and harm. Philosophy supplies the ethical and conceptual frameworks that technical systems require.

- "Philosophy is only for academia."

Philosophy graduates thrive in law, medicine, business, government, and technology—not just in classrooms.

Adaptability and Intellectual Humility
Philosophy fosters humility—the recognition that every viewpoint has limits. This mindset nurtures adaptability, allowing graduates to navigate changing industries and roles over their lifetimes.

Beyond Employment: philosophy and Purpose
Philosophy equips individuals to ask why, not only how. This deepens professional life with purpose and resilience, qualities increasingly vital in a world of rapid change and uncertainty.

Conclusion: A Foundation That Endures

Philosophy is not a luxury but a practical foundation for careers. Its training in reasoning, communication, and ethical judgment equips graduates to adapt, to lead, and to preserve coherence in institutions facing constant change. In law, medicine, business, policy, and technology, philosophy provides both the skills and the perspective that modern societies need.

Far from being outdated, philosophy offers one of the most resilient career foundations in the 21st century— preparing not only employable professionals but also wise leaders for an uncertain future.

CHAPTER 5 — CAREER PATHWAYS AND PROFESSIONAL OUTCOMES

Introduction: From Training to Trajectory

Philosophy is not an academic dead end—it is a foundation that expands into multiple professional directions. Where Chapter 4 focused on the pathways of upskilling, this chapter turns to outcomes. We examine how philosophy translates into careers, how graduates succeed in the labor market, and why the discipline produces resilient professionals across law, medicine, business, policy, technology, and beyond.

Critical Reasoning and Problem-Solving

Philosophy trains students to identify assumptions, expose flaws, and construct rigorous arguments. These habits of thought directly serve legal reasoning, policy debates, business negotiations, and strategy design. Employers consistently highlight critical thinking as among the most desired competencies, and philosophy provides it at the highest level.

Communication and Persuasion

Clarity of thought produces clarity of speech and writing. Philosophy graduates are skilled in framing complex problems for varied audiences, a capacity invaluable in leadership, consulting, law, and education. In an age of fragmented communication, the philosopher's ability to articulate coherent arguments is a professional advantage.

Ethical Judgment and Integrity

Modern careers increasingly require navigating questions of fairness and responsibility. Whether in medicine, finance, or corporate governance, decisions must be evaluated for legitimacy as well as efficiency. Philosophical training ensures professionals can weigh trade-offs and defend their choices on principled grounds.

Employment and Earnings

Contrary to popular myths, data show philosophy graduates fare strongly in the labor market:

- Unemployment Rates: Philosophy majors face unemployment levels comparable to or lower than those of many other large fields.
- Salary Trajectory: While entry-level salaries may appear modest, philosophy majors experience steady growth, often surpassing other humanities and social sciences by mid-career.
- Graduate Advantage: Many philosophy graduates pursue law, business, medicine, or advanced degrees, which magnify earnings potential while retaining philosophy's intellectual depth.

Graduate and Professional Success

Philosophy serves as a springboard to advanced study:

- Law: Philosophy majors regularly achieve top LSAT scores, reflecting their training in logic and argumentation.
- Medicine: Backgrounds in ethics and epistemology prepare graduates for complex clinical decisions.
- Business: MBA programs recruit philosophy graduates for their communication skills and strategic clarity.
- Academia: Philosophy itself remains a path for teaching and research, with questions that remain central to human progress.

The American Academy of Arts & Sciences confirms that philosophy majors consistently perform among the strongest on graduate entrance exams, reinforcing their versatility.

Addressing Common Critiques

"Philosophy is impractical."
Rebuttal: Philosophy provides universal skills—reasoning, communication, and ethical judgment—that transfer across sectors.

"Philosophy graduates face unemployment."
Rebuttal: Labor-market data shows relatively low unemployment and strong long-term career trajectories.

"Only STEM matters in the AI era."
Rebuttal: Without philosophical clarity, technical systems risk incoherence and harm. Philosophy supplies the ethical and conceptual frameworks that technology requires.

"Philosophy is only for academia."
Rebuttal: Philosophy graduates thrive in law, medicine, business, government, and technology—not just in classrooms.

Adaptability and Intellectual Humility

Philosophy fosters humility—the recognition that every viewpoint has limits. This mindset nurtures adaptability, allowing graduates to navigate changing industries and roles over their lifetimes.

Beyond Employment: Philosophy and Purpose

Philosophy equips individuals to ask why, not only how. This deepens professional life with purpose and resilience, qualities increasingly vital in a world of rapid change and uncertainty. Teams and institutions thrive when their leaders can clarify not only goals but also the values those goals serve.

Conclusion: Outcomes That Endure

Philosophy is not a luxury but a practical foundation for careers. Its training in reasoning, communication, and ethical judgment equips graduates to adapt, to lead, and to preserve coherence in institutions facing constant change. Far from being outdated, philosophy offers one of the most resilient career foundations in the 21st century—preparing not only employable professionals but also wise leaders for an uncertain future.

CHAPTER 6 — FROM CLASSROOM TO IMPACT: A PHILOSOPHY PLAYBOOK FOR REAL-WORLD RESULTS

■ Scope: This chapter converts the book's core claims into an actionable plan students and universities can use immediately. It focuses on methods, deliverables, and measurable outcomes rather than repeating arguments from earlier chapters.

The Transferable Core

Philosophy trains habits of mind that transfer: precise reading, structured reasoning, argument mapping, concept formation, and clarity under uncertainty. These habits are not merely academic; they are operational skills that improve outcomes in law, policy, business, research, engineering teams, and public communication. The more explicit you make these skills—and the more you demonstrate them in sharable artifacts—the more value you create for employers and collaborators.

The core practices to develop continuously are:

• Problem framing: defining the question, the assumptions, and the success criteria before proposing solutions.

• Evidence discipline: distinguishing data from inference; labeling confidence levels.

• Argument structure: using premises, warrants, and conclusions with explicit counter-arguments and failure conditions.

• Clarity and economy: writing and speaking so that a capable outsider can follow the reasoning the first time.

• Ethical foresight: identifying stakeholders, second-order effects, and off-ramps when things go wrong.

Build a Portfolio of Reason (PoR) (see Appendix A for details)

A Portfolio of Reason is a living, public-facing set of artifacts that makes your skills visible and verifiable. It is not a résumé substitute; it is evidence. Organize it around problems, not coursework. Each item should show the question, the method, the argument, the counter-case, and the result. Keep entries short and link to longer papers where needed. (see Appendix A for details)

Research and Data Literacy (Without the Pitfalls)

Good research starts with scope control and source integrity. Avoid over-claiming, and separate description from evaluation. Use peer-reviewed sources, recognized handbooks, and primary data where possible. When you must use secondary summaries, label them as such. The following operating procedures align with our protocol:

Communicating Across Disciplines

Interdisciplinary fluency is a comparative advantage of philosophy. You will often be the first person in the room to notice that two teams are using the same word differently. To communicate effectively across fields:

• Define terms upfront and translate them into the vocabulary of your audience (legal, engineering, policy, finance).

• Show your work: include a short appendix with argument maps, assumptions, and alternative models.

• Use working examples rather than abstractions—e.g., a hiring policy, a loan underwriting rule, a lab protocol, or a product feature gate.

Logic in Technology and AI (kept proportionate)

This book is not an AI manual, but modern teams benefit when a philosopher clarifies problem framing, assumptions, and error costs. Appropriate contributions include:

• Risk reasoning: distinguishing reversible from irreversible errors and selecting guardrails accordingly.

• Specification hygiene: writing plain-language versions of requirements so non-specialists can validate whether the model or system meets the intent.

• Evaluation discipline: pre-committing to success and failure criteria and reporting both; avoiding metric shopping after results arrive.

Ethics as Design, Not showmanship

Ethics is not an appendix to bolt on at the end. Treat it as part of the design space. Convert values into constraints and tests:

• Stakeholder table: who is affected, how, and what constitutes harm or benefit for each group.

• Second-order effects: what changes if adoption scales, incentives shift, or the environment reacts?

• Off-ramps: what will you do if the intervention under-performs or harms emerge? Plan reversal conditions in advance.

A Semester-by-Semester Roadmap

The following roadmap is a template. Adapt it to your institution's calendar. The aim is cumulative proof of skill.

First Semester

• Join one discussion-heavy course and one writing-intensive course; learn argument mapping and structured outlining.

• Create your PoR and publish your first decision brief. Label verification statuses on all claims.

• Attend two public talks (any field) and write 250-word analyses translating the talk's thesis into a premise-conclusion format.

Second Semester

• Take logic or critical thinking with a lab component (problem sets, case analysis).

• Publish one ethics memo on a real policy or product; include stakeholder table and off-ramps.

• Shadow a research group, clinic, or lab for a day; write a methods note on how they validate claims.

Third Semester

• Team project: partner with a club or local organization to frame a decision, produce options, and deliver a brief.

• Practice cross-disciplinary translation by co-authoring with a non-philosophy student.

• Submit to an undergraduate journal or conference; incorporate reviewer feedback as an appendix in your PoR.

Fourth Semester

• Elective in an adjacent field (economics, computer science, biology, public policy).

• Develop an evaluation plan for a small initiative (e.g., a tutoring program); pre-register success criteria.

• Conduct a second-order effects analysis for the initiative, specifying monitoring triggers and off-ramps.

Fifth Semester

• Internship or practicum emphasizing structured analysis and writing. Produce at least two public-safe artifacts.

• Guest lecture or workshop for a first-year seminar on reasoning methods; collect structured feedback.

• Begin a capstone plan; identify a mentor inside or outside your department.

Sixth Semester

• Capstone mid-point review: stress-test your thesis with a counter-case day where peers only argue the other side.

• Volunteer as a logic or writing coach for a campus group; document outcomes with before/after samples.

• Compile a short 'methods handbook' for your PoR (checklists for framing, verification, and evaluation).

Seventh Semester

• Advanced seminar tying your capstone to an external domain (law, science, business, public service).

• Public showcase: a 10-minute talk and a 2-page handout targeted to a general audience.

• Apply to fellowships, competitions, or graduate programs with tailored decision briefs rather than generic statements.

Eighth Semester

• Final capstone with transparent method, data, and verification logs.

• Portfolio audit: remove weak artifacts; mark all claims Verified/Pending; ensure date/version lock for sources.

• Exit interview with two mentors (inside and outside philosophy) to translate your work into role-relevant language.

Programmatic Recommendations for Departments

Universities can reinforce these practices with minimal cost by integrating them into existing structures:

• Portfolio requirement: one artifact per month across four categories (decision briefs, ethics memos, argument maps, methods notes).

• Verification workshops: hands-on sessions using real claims to practice the Verification Chain and Contextual Integrity Checks.

• Cross-disciplinary studios: mixed-major teams that solve a scoped problem and present to a community stakeholder.

• Feedback forms with rubrics: clarity, structure, verification, counter-case quality, and audience fitness.

• Capstone showcases: 10-minute talks to a public audience with Q&A designed for cross-examination of assumptions.

Simplified Summary

This chapter is a how-to guide. Build a public portfolio that shows how you think. Each piece should include your question, your steps, your sources, and what would change your mind. Use checklists to frame problems and verify facts. Practice explaining your ideas to people outside your field. Measure improvement by comparing early work to later work, by collecting feedback, and by trying real-world projects. Avoid big, vague claims. Let your artifacts prove your skills.

Conclusion — A Call to Action for the AI Age

Philosophy is not fading; it is rising in importance. The challenges of the AI age demand clarity, ethics, and philosophy—skills that philosophy uniquely provides. If universities want graduates who can reason across domains, build trustworthy technologies, and lead with integrity, philosophy must be central, not peripheral.

For universities: integrate philosophers into AI labs, data-science programs, and policy institutes. Expand courses in logic, epistemology, and philosophy of mind alongside machine learning and human-computer interaction. Evaluate AI curricula for ethical coherence, not only technical coverage.

For students: pair your philosophical training with targeted technical skills. Learn to prototype, code, analyze data, and design systems—but let philosophy govern your standards of reasoning and responsibility. The future needs thinkers who are both rigorous and humane.

Philosophy is the hidden power shaping the next generation of thinkers. Treat it as essential training for the AI age—and build a world worthy of intelligence.

Notes

4) EU AI Act — Regulation (EU) 2024/1689: human-oversight and risk-management requirements for high-risk AI. https://digital-strategy.ec.europa.eu/en/policies/regulatory-framework-ai

3) NIST, Artificial Intelligence Risk Management Framework (AI RMF 1.0), January 2023. https://doi.org/10.6028/NIST.AI.100-1

2) American Academy of Arts & Sciences, Humanities Indicators — Employment Status of Humanities Majors (2021 update and related profiles). https://www.amacad.org/humanities-indicators/workforce/employment-status-humanities-majors

1) Federal Reserve Bank of New York, "The Labor Market for Recent College Graduates" — Quarterly Highlights for 2025:Q2 report recent-grad unemployment ~5.3%. https://www.newyorkfed.org/research/college-labor-market

CHAPTER 7 — PHILOSOPHY AS MEANING AND PURPOSE

Throughout this book we have traced philosophy's roles in logic, ethics, governance, interdisciplinary work, and career development. At its deepest level, however, philosophy is not about employability or technical fluency—it is about philosophy. philosophy concerns more than information; it touches purpose, value, dignity, and identity. Where science explains how things work, and technology shows what can be built, philosophy insists on asking why. The ability to ask and answer the question of 'why' is a distinctly human power—one that no automated system can assume for us without loss.

1) The Limits of Machines on "Why"

Modern AI systems excel at pattern recognition, prediction, and optimization. Large language models compose essays and summarize documents; neural networks detect disease markers and guide vehicles. But when asked, "Why should I live a good life?" or "Why is fairness preferable to cruelty?", such systems offer recombinations of human texts rather than self-grounded reasons. They do not know or value the answers—they model them.

Philosophy's role in cultivating meaning is especially critical in times of cultural transition. Societies undergoing rapid technological shifts often experience disorientation: old frameworks no longer suffice, yet new ones remain untested. In such moments, philosophy functions as a stabilizing compass, equipping individuals to preserve coherence while engaging with change. By framing new experiences against enduring questions of justice, dignity, and identity, philosophy anchors transformation in principles that safeguard human worth.

Philosophy clarifies this gap. As Immanuel Kant argued in the Critique of Practical Reason (1788), moral obligation is not derived from empirical observation alone but from reason's own law. Likewise, Aristotle's Nicomachean Ethics treats human flourishing (eudaimonia) as a life of deliberate reflection about ends, not mere habit or impulse. These are claims about normativity—about what ought to be the case—not just about what is. AI, however powerful, operates within objectives humans specify; it does not originate ends.

2) Purpose Before Performance

Education that integrates meaning does more than prepare students for careers; it prepares them for citizenship and leadership. Philosophical study helps students articulate not only what they want to do, but why they want to do it, and how their goals contribute to a broader human community. This cultivation of purpose enriches both professional and civic life, fostering graduates who approach responsibility not merely as tasks but as opportunities to serve human flourishing.

Algorithms optimize against stated goals; philosophy interrogates whether the goals are worth pursuing. This difference matters in every domain:

• Law: Are we aiming at retribution, rehabilitation, deterrence, or restoration when we say 'justice'? Policies change depending on which meaning we adopt.

Another dimension of philosophy's contribution lies in helping individuals and communities navigate tragedy. When confronted with loss, injustice, or suffering, technical solutions can only address part of the need. Philosophy provides a vocabulary for grief, resilience, and renewal. Thinkers from the Stoics to Viktor Frankl have shown that meaning is often forged most powerfully in the crucible of adversity. This perspective allows individuals to respond to hardship with dignity rather than despair.

• Medicine: Is prolonging life always better than allowing natural death with dignity? What does 'benefit' mean for a terminal patient?

• Business: How should profit be balanced against responsibility to workers, communities, and the environment? What counts as a 'good' outcome beyond quarterly metrics?

Modern workplaces increasingly demand leaders who can balance efficiency with vision. Here philosophy distinguishes between intelligence—the ability to execute tasks—and wisdom—the capacity to evaluate ends. Leaders formed by philosophical training recognize that metrics and profits, while important, cannot be the sole measures of success. They ask whether the organization's goals align with justice, sustainability, and human dignity. In doing so, they elevate performance into purpose.

Philosophy keeps performance aligned with purpose. Without it, institutions drift toward technique without meaning.

3) Identity in an Age of Technology

Philosophy also deepens dialogue across traditions by inviting comparison between cultural frameworks of meaning. For example, Western conceptions of autonomy differ from Confucian ideals of harmony, yet both illuminate essential aspects of human dignity. By studying and synthesizing such traditions, philosophers create the conditions for global cooperation without erasing cultural difference. In a world increasingly interconnected, this comparative perspective is indispensable.

As machines simulate conversation, generate images, and outperform humans on numerous analytic tasks, many people ask what remains uniquely human. Philosophy answers: the capacity to situate ourselves within a horizon of meaning. Martin Heidegger described humans as beings who care about their own being (Dasein), and Viktor Frankl showed that survival and dignity in the harshest conditions depend on perceived purpose. Calculating systems do not experience care, aspiration, or transcendence; persons do.

Educating for identity therefore entails more than skill. It includes time-tested practices of reflection: examining assumptions, articulating values, and committing to life projects that express them.

In governance, philosophy reminds policymakers that legitimacy requires more than compliance. Laws must reflect coherent principles that citizens can recognize as just. When governments fail to ground their policies in meaning—reducing decisions to mere expedience—they risk losing public trust. Philosophical clarity ensures that governance is more than administration; it is stewardship of values that transcend any single generation.

4) Wisdom Versus Intelligence

Intelligence—human or artificial—refers to the ability to acquire and apply knowledge to solve problems. Wisdom is the capacity to judge what is good, right, and worth pursuing in the first place. Contemporary AI grows rapidly in problem-solving intelligence, but it lacks wisdom. It does not evaluate ends; it optimizes means. Philosophy cultivates wisdom: the habit of weighing long-term consequences, balancing competing goods, and acting from principled reasons rather than narrow objectives.

Technology provides another vivid arena for philosophy's guidance. As artificial intelligence, biotechnology, and genetic editing reshape human possibility, the central question is not only what these tools can accomplish but what they mean for our identity. By clarifying concepts such as dignity, autonomy, and flourishing, philosophy helps ensure that innovation serves humanity rather than undermining it. Without such clarity, technical advances risk drifting into incoherence or exploitation.

5) Education for Meaning

Universities understandably emphasize employability, yet a solely utilitarian curriculum risks losing the very soul of education. A philosophy curriculum oriented toward meaning prepares graduates to:

Even at the personal level, philosophy equips individuals with practices that sustain meaning. Daily reflection, argument mapping, and value clarification exercises transform abstract ideals into lived habits. These practices strengthen resilience against distraction and nihilism by grounding everyday choices in coherence. Students who engage philosophy in this way discover that meaning is not an abstract luxury but a practical resource for navigating life's complexity.

• Navigate ambiguity without despair, resisting the allure of simplistic answers.
• Examine personal and cultural assumptions with intellectual humility.
• Articulate coherent accounts of justice, beauty, and truth, then test those accounts against criticism.
• Translate values into action through policies, designs, and leadership decisions.

Such formation strengthens careers rather than opposing them: teams follow leaders who can explain what work is for, not only how to do it.

Finally, philosophy cultivates the courage to confront uncertainty. While other disciplines often promise definitive answers, philosophy models intellectual humility by showing how deep questions invite exploration rather than closure. This humility is not weakness but strength: it fosters adaptability, openness, and resilience in the face of change. In an age where rapid technological and cultural shifts are inevitable, the courage to live with questions may be the most practical skill of all.

6) Meaning in Governance

Debates about AI regulation often present as technical: thresholds, audits, documentation. Underneath are questions of meaning: what values a society aims to preserve. For example, the European Union's AI Act (2024/1689) embeds human oversight and risk management for high-risk systems, and the U.S. NIST AI Risk Management Framework (2023) emphasizes accountability and trustworthiness. These frameworks presuppose philosophical commitments: that dignity, fairness, and responsibility limit what even efficient systems should do.

Philosophical clarity prevents governance from collapsing into technocracy. It keeps ethical terms substantive rather than rhetorical and invites public reason—open justification that citizens can evaluate.

7) Practices That Build Meaning

The following exercises convert Chapter 7's ideas into action. They can be implemented in seminars, labs, or civic settings:

A. Ethical Specification: Before a project begins, write a one-page 'purpose specification' that defines the good you aim to advance, the harms you refuse to cause, and the trade-offs you will monitor. Revisit quarterly.

B. Stakeholder Table with Off-Ramps: Identify who is affected, how, and the conditions under which you would pause or reverse deployment. Commit to them publicly.

C. Counter-Case Day: Present the strongest argument against your preferred policy or design. Record what would change your mind (falsifiers).

D. Reflection Capsule: 300–500 words on what most changed your mind this term—and why. Archive these in a Portfolio of Reason. (see Appendix A for details)

E. Meaning Audit: For any recurring decision, ask: What is the purpose of this process? What value is being preserved? What would count as betrayal of that value?

8) Conclusion: Meaning as Humanity's Safeguard

Philosophy is the discipline of meaning—the study of the 'why' behind the 'how'. In a world saturated with intelligent machines, humans must cultivate wisdom to remain authors of purpose. Philosophy equips students, professionals, and leaders to wrestle with identity and value, preserving what is uniquely human while directing intelligence toward humane ends. Without philosophy, intelligence risks becoming blind power; with philosophy, intelligence becomes wise.

Simplified Summary

This chapter explains why philosophy matters when machines get smart. AI can solve problems, but it cannot decide what is worth doing. Philosophy helps people define goals, balance values like fairness and dignity, and take responsibility for choices. In school, students should learn habits that build meaning: question assumptions, explain their values, listen to criticism, and plan off-ramps if a policy causes harm. Good rules and laws depend on these ideas. Philosophy does not replace technology—it guides it so that power is used for the good.

References

Aristotle, Nicomachean Ethics. ca. 4th century BCE.

Frankl, Viktor. Man's Search for Meaning. Beacon Press, 1946.

Heidegger, Martin. Being and Time. Niemeyer, 1927.

Kant, Immanuel. Critique of Practical Reason. 1788.

Leibniz, Gottfried Wilhelm. Monadology (1714); Discourse on Metaphysics (1686).

European Union. AI Act (Regulation (EU) 2024/1689).

National Institute of Standards and Technology. AI Risk Management Framework (AI RMF 1.0), 2023.

CHAPTER 8 — PHILOSOPHY AS SOCIETY'S COMPASS

Throughout this book, we have traced philosophy's contributions to logic, ethics, governance, interdisciplinary problem solving, career development, and meaning. Yet its most enduring role is broader still: philosophy acts as society's compass. It not only equips individuals for professional success but also orients communities and civilizations toward coherence, justice, and purpose. Without this compass, technical power risks drifting into misuse, and social systems collapse into fragmentation. With philosophy, society preserves the capacity to ask not only "What is possible?" but "Where should we go?"

Philosophy as Cultural Foundation

Civilizations rise and endure through their shared commitments to justice, knowledge, and meaning. Philosophy clarifies these commitments by providing the categories through which societies understand themselves. The Greek polis, the Enlightenment, and the constitutional democracies of modernity were all grounded in philosophical reflection.

Today's societies face similar challenges of direction: navigating globalization, climate change, artificial intelligence, and cultural pluralism. Each challenge contains not only technical problems but also philosophical ones:

- Globalization asks: what principles of justice govern across borders?
- Climate change asks: what obligations do we have to future generations?

- AI and biotechnology ask: what boundaries should constrain human innovation?
- Cultural pluralism asks: how can diverse traditions coexist while preserving dignity for all?

In each case, philosophy provides not answers ready-made, but a framework for reasoned deliberation—ensuring societies orient themselves by coherent principles rather than expedience.

The Compass in Governance

Governance is more than rule-making; it is orientation toward the good. Technical regulation alone cannot secure legitimacy. Citizens must perceive that laws express justice, fairness, and accountability. Here philosophy ensures that governance does not reduce to procedure.

- Constitutional frameworks: Locke's social contract and Montesquieu's separation of powers continue to guide how authority is balanced.
- Democratic values: John Stuart Mill's defense of liberty and Habermas's insistence on communicative rationality preserve freedom against coercion.
- Contemporary policy: Ethical debates on surveillance, biotechnology, and AI regulation hinge on concepts of dignity, rights, and human flourishing.

Philosophy ensures that when governments legislate, they legislate not only efficiently but also justly.

Guiding Science and Technology

Science excels at discovering what is, and technology at creating what can be. But philosophy alone insists on asking what ought to be. Without this compass, knowledge risks misuse and innovation risks exploitation.

Historical cases illustrate the point:

- Nuclear physics gave rise to atomic energy and weapons. Philosophers like Hannah Arendt warned of the moral stakes of wielding such power without deliberation.
- Biotechnology offers cures and enhancements but also raises questions of eugenics and inequality. Bioethics, rooted in philosophical traditions, prevents progress from sliding into abuse.
- Artificial intelligence promises efficiency but risks bias, opacity, and disconnection from human ends. Philosophical clarity on justice, accountability, and meaning ensures AI develops in service of humanity.

Science and technology extend human power; philosophy orients that power toward the good.

Philosophy as a Unifying Language

Modern societies are fragmented into specialized disciplines, interest groups, and political divisions. Philosophy provides a shared language for dialogue across these divides. By clarifying concepts—justice, knowledge, fairness, autonomy—it allows competing perspectives to converse rather than clash.

In universities, this role appears in the way philosophy bridges STEM and the humanities. In civic life, it appears when debates on policy return to principles citizens can recognize and evaluate. In global forums, philosophy fosters intercultural reasoning that seeks coherence rather than dominance.

The Ethical Compass in Crisis

Crises test the moral compass of societies. Pandemics, wars, and economic upheavals force rapid decisions with long-term consequences. Philosophy equips leaders to navigate these moments without losing sight of first principles.

- During pandemics, utilitarian reasoning balances public health with individual rights, while deontological reasoning guards against coercion.
- During conflicts, just war theory clarifies when defense is legitimate and when aggression violates human dignity.
- During economic recessions, distributive justice theories inform how burdens and benefits should be shared.

In each case, philosophy prevents crisis management from devolving into mere survival tactics. It sustains moral orientation even under pressure.

Education for Civic Responsibility

If philosophy is society's compass, it must be cultivated broadly, not confined to specialists. Philosophy education fosters the civic virtues that sustain democracy: intellectual humility, critical dialogue, and ethical judgment.

Students trained in philosophy become citizens capable of evaluating rhetoric, resisting manipulation, and contributing to collective reasoning. In a world saturated with misinformation, this civic literacy is essential. Without it, public discourse risks collapse into partisanship and noise.

Meaning, Community, and the Future

Earlier chapters showed how philosophy anchors personal meaning. At the societal level, it anchors shared identity. Communities cohere not only through laws and markets but through shared narratives about justice, progress, and destiny. Philosophy articulates and critiques these narratives, ensuring they remain open to rational revision rather than hardened into dogma.

Looking forward, global challenges will demand a renewed compass:

- Climate responsibility requires principles of intergenerational justice.
- Technological integration requires ethical limits and safeguards.
- Cultural diversity requires frameworks for pluralism without relativism.

Philosophy will remain indispensable as societies confront these frontiers.

CHAPTER 9 — PHILOSOPHY AS PREPARATION FOR LIFE

Philosophy prepares people for life not by handing down doctrines, but by cultivating habits of mind that work under pressure: clear framing, disciplined evidence, principled judgment, and the courage to revise beliefs when facts change. Where earlier chapters showed philosophy's value for careers and governance, this chapter turns explicitly to everyday practice. It offers a practical blueprint for using philosophical methods to navigate uncertainty, relationships, work, money, civic life, and purpose—the ordinary arenas where character and reason matter most. The aim is not to add yet another list of life hacks, but to show how the same durable methods— framing, verification, counter-case analysis, and ethical foresight—translate into resilient action.

1) Orientation: Why "Preparation for Life" Is Philosophical

Life is a stream of decisions made under uncertainty. Philosophy trains decision-makers to slow down at the right moments—to identify assumptions, ask what would count as disconfirming evidence, and articulate the values at stake before acting. This is not abstraction for its own sake; it is the operating system of wise action. The core stance is humility with discipline: humility that recognizes limits and bias, discipline that insists on methods strong enough to withstand criticism.

2) Decision-Making Under Uncertainty

Good decisions come from good preparation. The following portable tools implement that preparation in daily life:

• Problem framing: Write a one-sentence statement of the decision. List the key assumptions. Define the success criteria in plain language.

• Base rates before anecdotes: Ask what typically happens in comparable situations before reviewing vivid recent stories.

• Expected-value thinking: Consider both probability and magnitude of outcomes rather than focusing only on best- or worst-case.

• Pre-mortem: Imagine that your decision failed. List the most plausible reasons. Adjust the plan now to address them.

• Counter-case day: Briefly argue the strongest case against your preferred option. Note what evidence would flip your view.

• Time-boxed experimentation: When stakes permit, run a reversible trial first. Prefer decisions that are easy to unwind.

These methods do not eliminate uncertainty; they convert it from a fog into a map with known blind spots. They echo research in judgment and forecasting that shows structured methods outperform intuition alone over time.

3) Resilience and Character

Philosophy distinguishes between what is within our control and what is not, directing energy toward the former. Three practices operationalize this stance:

• Value commitments: Write the two or three virtues you intend to practice this season (e.g., fairness, courage, fidelity to evidence). Tie weekly actions to them.

• Adversity scripts: Pre-plan language for setbacks— what you will say to yourself and to others when a plan fails. Scripts prevent panic and preserve integrity under stress.

• Reflection capsules: 300–500 words on what changed your mind this month and why. Archive these to document intellectual growth.

These practices build the muscle of principled persistence—steadfast without becoming rigid.

4) Communication and Persuasion

Persuasion begins with accurate understanding. Philosophical dialogue requires charity (state the other view as its advocates would) and structure (separate claims, reasons, and evidence). Practical steps:

• Begin meetings with a shared definition of the problem and success criteria.

• Use argument maps for contentious issues: claims → reasons → evidence → counter-reasons.

• Distinguish description from evaluation; do not smuggle judgments into facts.

• Seek disconfirmation actively by inviting the best objections. This signals seriousness and reduces downstream conflict.

5) Ethical Living: From Values to Design

Convert values into constraints and tests before you act:

• Purpose specification: In one page, write the good you intend to advance, the harms you refuse to cause, and trade-offs you will monitor.

• Stakeholder table with off-ramps: Who is affected? How? Under what conditions will you pause or reverse the plan?

• Transparency by default: Document decisions and the reasons behind them so others can verify your integrity.

These devices translate ideals into procedures that withstand scrutiny.

6) Financial Reasoning for Philosophers

Financial choices are ethical and epistemic choices before they are numerical ones. A philosophical approach emphasizes:

• Time horizons: Match decisions to the time you actually have. Long-horizon goals tolerate volatility; near-term needs do not.

• Risk clarity: Separate risk you are paid to take from risk you are not (fees, leverage, concentration).

• Error costs: Prefer reversible experiments for unproven ideas; automate good habits (saving, bill-pay) to remove willpower from the loop.

• Simplicity as a virtue: Complex plans accumulate hidden assumptions. The right level of simplicity preserves robustness.

This is not investment advice; it is a method for thinking clearly about money in service of a coherent life.

7) Civic Literacy and Public Reason

Democracy depends on citizens who can evaluate claims without succumbing to spectacle. Philosophy trains this literacy:

• Source triage: Prefer peer-reviewed research, official statistics, and primary documents over commentary. Label verification status.

• Concept hygiene: Define fairness, harm, and rights explicitly; do not let slogans substitute for reasons.

• Pluralism with standards: Treat disagreement as normal while insisting on evidence and logic. A society that argues well keeps power accountable.

8) Relationships and Collaboration

Philosophy is not solitary. Working with others requires disciplined listening and trustworthy speech:

• Ask repeat-back questions: "Can I restate your view to be sure I have it right?"

• Commitments with check-ins: Turn promises into dated checkpoints; publish them to reduce ambiguity.

• Generous attributions: Prefer error to malice when interpreting others' mistakes unless evidence forces otherwise.

These habits lower friction and preserve goodwill, allowing serious work to proceed.

9) Lifelong Learning and the Portfolio of Reason (PoR)

A Portfolio of Reason makes your growth auditable. Organize it around problems solved, not credentials obtained. Each artifact should show the question, the method, the counter-case, and the result. Include verification logs—sources consulted, claims labeled as Verified or Pending, and date/version locks for studies used. Over time, the PoR becomes evidence of character as much as competence.

10) A 12-Week Practical Guide

Week 1–2: Build your decision template (framing, base rates, pre-mortem). Run it on one real choice. Archive results.

Week 3–4: Write one ethics memo on a personal or community decision. Include stakeholder table and off-ramps.

Week 5–6: Conduct a counter-case day on a conviction you hold. Record what would change your mind.

Week 7–8: Publish a 2-page decision brief with links to sources and a verification log.

Week 9–10: Teach a mini-workshop to peers on argument mapping; collect feedback forms.

Week 11–12: Synthesize: a 3-page 'methods handbook' for yourself. Commit to quarterly updates.

11) Illustrative Success Profiles

• The Analyst-Advocate: A graduate pairs a PoR with internships at a public-interest law center, translating ethics into policy briefs. Outcome: an entry role in regulatory analysis with responsibility for stakeholder engagement.

• The Builder-Communicator: A philosophy major cross-trains in data analysis and helps a nonprofit evaluate programs. Outcome: a program manager role, promoted for clarity and integrity in decision reporting.

• The Educator-Connector: A student leads a campus seminar on reasoning methods and builds community partnerships. Outcome: admission to a policy master's program with funding based on demonstrated civic impact.

These are composites, not case studies; they illustrate how philosophical methods convert into trust and opportunity.

Conclusion: A Coherent Life

Preparation for life means building a character that reasons well, keeps promises, and stays oriented to the good. Philosophy provides the methods and the motives for such lives. Methods—because it supplies tools that withstand scrutiny. Motives—because it orients us toward purposes worthy of intelligence. With disciplined practice, these habits compound into resilience and trust—the durable advantages of a philosophical education.

Simplified Summary

This chapter turns philosophy into daily tools. Before deciding, define the problem, check typical outcomes, and run a quick pre-mortem. Practice a 'counter-case day' to stress-test your views. Convert values into action by writing a one-page purpose statement and a stakeholder table with off-ramps. Use simple, reversible trials when stakes are low; document what you learn. Build a Portfolio of Reason that shows your questions, methods, and evidence. These habits make you steadier under pressure, clearer with others, and better at choosing what really matters.

Philosophy ensures that when complex systems are modeled, their ethical and human dimensions remain visible. Systems thinking without philosophical oversight risks optimizing technical efficiency at the expense of long-term sustainability and justice. Philosophy reframes models to incorporate values, accountability, and resilience, ensuring that complex systems serve coherent human purposes.

Education gains depth when students learn to integrate insights across fields. Philosophy equips learners with meta-cognitive tools to bridge science, technology, and humanities. This preparation makes students adaptable, capable of navigating uncertainty, and skilled at connecting abstract concepts to practical contexts.

Media narratives shape public perception of science, technology, and governance. Philosophers contribute by clarifying terms, debunking false equivalences, and highlighting assumptions. Their role in communication helps societies resist manipulation, rebuild trust, and make informed collective decisions.

Healthcare is not only a technical practice but also a humanistic one. Philosophy ensures that autonomy, dignity, and justice remain central, even as advanced diagnostic tools proliferate. By balancing efficiency with compassion, philosophy prevents healthcare from devolving into a purely mechanistic enterprise.

Diplomacy often involves reconciling conflicting worldviews. Philosophy provides the conceptual language for justice, sovereignty, and legitimacy across cultures. It enables nations to find common ground while respecting difference, making it an indispensable tool for peace and cooperation.

Modern business faces pressure to balance profit with fairness and sustainability. Philosophical reasoning helps organizations articulate ethical priorities, anticipate long-term risks, and preserve trust among stakeholders. This role is especially critical in times of crisis, when short-term gain may tempt abandonment of responsibility.

Technology embeds values, often invisibly. Philosophers help design teams recognize these value-laden assumptions and guide choices that respect fairness, transparency, and dignity. This proactive integration of ethics into design prevents downstream harms and increases trust in innovation.

CHAPTER 10— PHILOSOPHY AS GUIDANCE FOR PARENTS AND COUNSELORS

Philosophy is not only an academic pursuit for students and scholars; it is also a vital guidepost for parents and counselors who shape the choices young people make about their education and their future. In a world where career paths change rapidly and technologies evolve faster than curricula, philosophy provides a stabilizing framework. It grounds students not only in employability but also in purpose and resilience, helping them face uncertainty with clarity and confidence.

Parents often worry whether their children's education will prepare them for meaningful work. Guidance counselors, likewise, must help students navigate between practical demands and deeper aspirations. Philosophy equips students with skills—critical thinking, ethical judgment, and clear communication—that remain valuable across all professions. Unlike technical training that can become outdated, these capacities endure, adapting to new challenges as industries transform.

Counselors can emphasize that philosophy majors are not choosing an impractical path but are instead developing a universal toolkit. Whether students go into law, medicine, business, technology, or public service, their grounding in philosophy allows them to connect disciplines, clarify assumptions, and lead with integrity. Parents, when reassured of this, can support their children's choices with confidence rather than fear.

Beyond careers, philosophy helps young people prepare for life's broader challenges—decisions about relationships, finances, civic responsibility, and personal values. By cultivating habits of reasoning and resilience, philosophy equips students to face adversity without losing coherence. For parents, this means raising children who can stand firm in their values while remaining adaptable to change.

Guidance counselors can also highlight the role philosophy plays in building character and purpose. Students trained to reflect on questions of justice, fairness, and dignity are better prepared to lead organizations, communities, and families. In times of uncertainty or crisis, these qualities matter as much as technical expertise. Parents will find that philosophy fosters maturity, empathy, and long-term vision in their children.

It is important to remember that philosophy is not a retreat from the real world but an engagement with it at the deepest level. By pairing philosophical training with practical skills, students gain both adaptability and direction. Counselors who frame philosophy this way help students and families see it as a foundation rather than a limitation, and parents can encourage their children to pursue it without hesitation.

A Pathway for Parents Themselves
Small Starts for Parents

While this book is directed primarily toward helping students, it is worth noting that philosophy can be just as valuable for parents themselves. Life today moves quickly, and most parents face demanding schedules. Still, if time allows, exploring philosophy directly—whether by taking a course at a local college, joining a community lecture, or simply reading a few well-chosen works—can enrich their own lives.

Philosophy sharpens reasoning, deepens perspective, and fosters resilience. Parents who engage with it personally will not only see the benefits for themselves but will also be better equipped to support their children's intellectual journey. More than an academic subject, philosophy is a lifelong companion that offers clarity in decision-making, strength in adversity, and meaning in daily life.

For many parents, this engagement may begin with small steps: reading accessible introductions, listening to podcasts that explore philosophical themes, or even joining discussion groups that meet in libraries or online forums. These modest efforts can quickly reveal that philosophy is not remote or abstract, but practical and deeply connected to the challenges of family, work, and community life.

Shared Language at Home

Parents who discover philosophy for themselves often find that it becomes a shared language in the household. Conversations about fairness, justice, responsibility, or meaning take on greater depth, providing opportunities for connection between generations. In this way, philosophy does not simply prepare students for their future—it enriches the entire family's present.

Philosophy as a Bridge Across Generations
Understanding the Generational Gap

Parents and children often experience what is commonly called a "generational gap." At times, parents may feel uncertain about how to connect with their child's way of thinking, while children may struggle to express themselves clearly to their parents. Misunderstandings can easily escalate into conflict when neither side feels truly heard.

Reasoning Toward Harmony

Philosophy provides a bridge across that gap. It encourages both parents and children to slow down, examine assumptions, and approach dialogue with reason rather than impulse. By fostering habits of listening, questioning, and clarifying terms, philosophy helps families engage in meaningful discussion without turning differences into divisions. Agreement is not always necessary, but mutual understanding and respect become possible. In this way, philosophy creates the conditions for harmony rather than discord.

Ultimately, philosophy provides more than knowledge; it provides coherence. For parents and counselors, the message is clear: encouraging philosophy means preparing students not just for a job, but for a life of meaning, resilience, and leadership. In an age of rapid change, these are the qualities that will sustain young people and help them thrive in whatever path they choose.

Simplified Summary

This chapter is written for parents and counselors. It explains why philosophy is not only helpful for students choosing a major, but also useful for families. Philosophy builds skills that last: clear thinking, listening, and fair judgment. These skills make students stronger in school, careers, and life.

Parents are encouraged to see philosophy as practical, not abstract. It prepares students for many jobs, but more importantly it prepares them to live wisely. Even busy parents may benefit from exploring philosophy themselves, through classes, books, or community events. It can improve decision-making, reduce stress, and deepen understanding of life's choices.

Philosophy also helps close the generational gap between parents and children. Instead of arguments, families can practice reasoning together, hearing one another's views without anger. This does not always bring agreement, but it brings respect and harmony. In this way, philosophy supports not just education, but the strength of families and communities.

Suggested Reading for Parents and Counselors

James Miller, *Examined Lives: From Socrates to Nietzsche* (Farrar, Straus and Giroux, 2011) — A readable introduction to key philosophers and their lessons for everyday life.

Martha C. Nussbaum, *Cultivating Humanity: A Classical Defense of Reform in Liberal Education* (Harvard University Press, 1997) — Shows how philosophy enriches education and civic life.

Bertrand Russell, *The Problems of Philosophy* (Oxford University Press, 1912/1997) — A classic short work introducing core philosophical questions in accessible language.

Viktor E. Frankl, *Man's Search for Meaning* (Beacon Press, 1946) — A profound reflection on purpose, resilience, and human dignity.

Tom Morris, *If Aristotle Ran General Motors: The New Soul of Business* (Henry Holt, 1997) — Demonstrates how philosophical principles apply to leadership and daily decision-making.

Lou Marinoff, *Plato, Not Prozac!* (HarperCollins, 1999) — Explains how philosophy can be used as a practical guide for solving personal and family challenges.

Chapter 11: Philosophers Who Shaped the Understanding of Mind and Reality

In order to understand why philosophy remains essential to higher education and to the broader human quest for meaning, it is helpful to look at the thinkers whose ideas continue to resonate through the centuries. The following survey presents a selection of philosophers from both the classical and modern eras, whose work in metaphysics, philosophy of mind, law, and science has profoundly influenced the intellectual landscape. Their ideas not only provide historical context but also reinforce the arguments developed throughout this book, demonstrating philosophy's enduring relevance.

Gottfried Wilhelm Leibniz

Leibniz (1646–1716) was a German polymath and philosopher whose contributions to metaphysics and logic remain pivotal. His Monadology advanced the idea that reality is composed of simple, indivisible substances he called monads, each reflecting the universe from its unique perspective (Leibniz, 1714/1991). This concept provided a way to reconcile individuality with unity, suggesting a pre-established harmony undergirding all things. His Principle of Sufficient Reason further established that nothing exists without an explanation, offering a metaphysical grounding for rational inquiry (Leibniz, 1686/1991).

Leibniz's influence reaches beyond philosophy into mathematics and science, where he co-invented calculus and laid the foundations for symbolic logic (Leibniz, 1989). For philosophy of mind, his rejection of material reductionism and his view that consciousness arises from structured realities prefigure modern debates about consciousness and computation. His work remains

73

especially significant for those exploring metaphysical accounts of mind and reality.

René Descartes

Descartes (1596–1650), often called the father of modern philosophy, is best known for his declaration, 'Cogito, ergo sum' ('I think, therefore I am'). His dualistic philosophy separated mind and body, establishing the mind as an immaterial substance distinct from the physical body (Descartes, 1641/1996). This framework created the foundation for modern philosophy of mind by clearly articulating the problem of how consciousness and matter interact.

While Cartesian dualism has been critiqued and reinterpreted, Descartes's insistence on doubt, rational inquiry, and the clarity of self-awareness reshaped metaphysical inquiry (Cottingham, 1992). His ideas remain central to ongoing debates about consciousness, identity, and the relationship between subjective experience and physical reality.

Immanuel Kant

Kant (1724–1804) revolutionized philosophy by arguing that our experience of the world is structured by innate categories of the mind. In his Critique of Pure Reason, he distinguished between phenomena (things as they appear to us) and noumena (things as they are in themselves) (Kant, 1781/1998). This distinction reshaped metaphysics, suggesting that while human knowledge is limited to phenomena, reason itself plays a constitutive role in shaping reality as experienced.

Kant's work provided a bridge between rationalism and empiricism and influenced virtually every subsequent branch of philosophy (Guyer, 2006). For philosophy of mind, his account of the mind's structuring role highlights how consciousness participates in constructing experience, a theme that resonates strongly with contemporary metaphysical discussions of mind and reality.

Aristotle

Aristotle (384–322 BCE), student of Plato and tutor to Alexander the Great, stands as one of the most influential figures in Western philosophy. His works in metaphysics, logic, and natural philosophy established foundational principles still used in philosophical discourse today (Aristotle, Metaphysics, trans. Ross, 1924). His concept of substance and causality shaped centuries of metaphysical inquiry, offering a systematic framework for understanding change, being, and purpose in nature.

Aristotle's emphasis on empirical observation and systematic categorization provided a basis for scientific thought as well as philosophical reasoning (Lear, 1988). His focus on the unity of form and matter in living beings continues to influence modern debates in philosophy of science and mind, reminding us that philosophy provides the groundwork upon which scientific understanding often rests.

John Locke

Locke (1632–1704), an English philosopher, was central to the development of empiricism and political theory. His theory of personal identity, based on continuity of consciousness, directly shaped discussions in philosophy of mind about selfhood and memory (Locke, 1690/1996). By grounding knowledge in experience, Locke provided a counterpoint to rationalism, emphasizing the role of sensory input and reflection in forming ideas.

Beyond metaphysics, Locke's work on law, governance, and human rights became a cornerstone of liberal political thought (Tully, 1993). His notion of natural rights and the social contract influenced modern constitutional democracy. In both philosophy of mind and law, Locke exemplifies how philosophy can shape not only abstract theory but also practical institutions of society.

Martin Heidegger

Heidegger (1889–1976), a German existentialist and phenomenologist, explored the question of Being in ways that redefined metaphysics. His magnum opus, Being and Time, sought to uncover the structures of human existence (Dasein) and its relation to time, mortality, and authenticity (Heidegger, 1927/1962). By shifting attention from abstract essences to lived experience, Heidegger reframed philosophy's task as clarifying what it means to be.

Though sometimes criticized for his obscurity, Heidegger's emphasis on phenomenology and existential analysis influenced fields as diverse as psychology, theology, and literary theory (Inwood, 2000). For philosophy of mind, his exploration of Being-in-the-world demonstrates how consciousness cannot be separated from context, embodiment, and temporality.

Gilbert Ryle

Ryle (1900–1976), an English philosopher, famously critiqued Cartesian dualism by dismissing it as a 'category mistake.' In The Concept of Mind, he argued against viewing the mind as a non-physical entity separate from the body, instead describing mental processes as dispositions and behaviors (Ryle, 1949/2000). His phrase 'the ghost in the machine' captured his rejection of metaphysical dualism.

Ryle's work helped shape analytic philosophy and behaviorism, reframing discussions of consciousness in terms of observable capacities and linguistic practices (Dennett, 1984). While later developments moved beyond his behaviorist leanings, his critique of dualism remains a central milestone in philosophy of mind.

John Searle

Searle (born 1932), an American philosopher, advanced influential arguments in philosophy of mind and language. His famous Chinese Room thought experiment challenged claims that computers could genuinely understand language or possess consciousness, arguing instead that syntax alone cannot produce semantics (Searle, 1980). This critique shaped debates in artificial intelligence and the philosophy of cognition.

Searle also developed a broader account of social reality, showing how collective intentionality and speech acts structure institutions and meaning (Searle, 1995). His work underscores how consciousness is not only a biological but also a social phenomenon, bridging metaphysical and practical concerns in philosophy.

Martha Nussbaum

Nussbaum (1947–), a contemporary philosopher, is best known for her capabilities approach, which integrates philosophy, law, and human rights. By emphasizing what individuals are able to do and to be, her work connects ancient ethical traditions with modern debates about justice, education, and social flourishing (Nussbaum, 2000). Her scholarship demonstrates how philosophy remains indispensable for shaping law and policy.

Nussbaum's thought illustrates how philosophy can respond to concrete human needs while maintaining rigorous theoretical foundations (Nussbaum, 2011). In a work that underscores philosophy's relevance to universities and society, her voice demonstrates how the discipline speaks not only to abstract truth but also to the structures of everyday life and justice.

Bibliography

Aristotle. Metaphysics. Translated by W. D. Ross. Oxford: Clarendon Press, 1924.

Cottingham, John. Descartes. Oxford: Blackwell, 1986.

Dennett, Daniel. Elbow Room: The Varieties of Free Will Worth Wanting. Cambridge: MIT Press, 1984.

Descartes, René. Meditations on First Philosophy. 1641. Translated by John Cottingham. Cambridge: Cambridge University Press, 1996.

Leibniz, Gottfried Wilhelm. Philosophical Essays. Translated and edited by Roger Ariew and Daniel Garber. Indianapolis: Hackett, 1989.

Guyer, Paul. Kant. New York: Routledge, 2006.

Heidegger, Martin. Being and Time. 1927. Translated by John Macquarrie and Edward Robinson. New York: Harper & Row, 1962.

Inwood, Michael. Heidegger: A Very Short Introduction. Oxford: Oxford University Press, 2000.

Kant, Immanuel. Critique of Pure Reason. 1781. Translated by Paul Guyer and Allen Wood. Cambridge: Cambridge University Press, 1998.

Leibniz, Gottfried Wilhelm. Discourse on Metaphysics and Other Essays. Translated by Daniel Garber and Roger Ariew. Indianapolis: Hackett, 1991.

Leibniz, Gottfried Wilhelm. The Principles of Philosophy, or, the Monadology (1714). In Philosophical Essays, translated and edited by Roger Ariew and Daniel Garber. Indianapolis: Hackett, 1989.

Lear, Jonathan. Aristotle: The Desire to Understand. Cambridge: Cambridge University Press, 1988.

Locke, John. An Essay Concerning Human Understanding. 1690. Edited by Peter H. Nidditch. Oxford: Clarendon Press, 1996.

Nussbaum, Martha. Women and Human Development: The Capabilities Approach. Cambridge: Cambridge University Press, 2000.

Nussbaum, Martha. Creating Capabilities. Cambridge: Harvard University Press, 2011.

Ryle, Gilbert. The Concept of Mind. 1949. Chicago: University of Chicago Press, 2000.

Searle, John. Minds, Brains, and Programs. Behavioral and Brain Sciences 3, no. 3 (1980): 417–457.

Searle, John. The Construction of Social Reality. New York: Free Press, 1995.

Tully, James. An Approach to Political Philosophy: Locke in Contexts. Cambridge: Cambridge University Press, 1993.

Appendix of Study and Discussion Questions
Chapter 1 — Philosophy as Conceptual Foundations

• What historical examples demonstrate how philosophy provided the foundation for science, law, or mathematics?

• How does logic continue to shape technology and computer science today?

• Do you think Artificial Intelligence can truly 'know' something, or is it limited to statistical inference? Defend your view.

• Why are epistemological questions still relevant in modern contexts such as medicine, governance, or AI?

Chapter 2 — Philosophy as Ethics and Governance

• How can utilitarianism and deontology lead to very different decisions in technology or AI policy? Provide an example.

• What are the strengths and limitations of virtue ethics when applied to AI or governance?

• How do cultural values influence governance frameworks in different regions (e.g., U.S., Europe, Japan)?

• What lessons from Plato's Republic or Aristotle's Politics remain relevant for governance today?

Chapter 3 — Philosophy as Interdisciplinary Problem Solving

• Why is philosophy often described as a 'translator' between disciplines?

• How can philosophical reasoning prevent costly errors in fields such as medicine or economics?

• In what ways does philosophical clarity help build trust in public communication?

• How does interdisciplinary thinking improve resilience in solving global problems such as climate change or pandemics?

Chapter 4 — The Upskilling Path for Philosophy Majors

• What does it mean to say that philosophy is a 'launchpad' for other disciplines?

• Which upskilling pathway (law, medicine, business, AI, etc.) do you find most interesting, and why?

• How does studying epistemology strengthen careers in data science or policy analysis?

• Why is ethical training increasingly valued in business, healthcare, and governance?

Chapter 5 — Career Pathways and Professional Outcomes

• What evidence challenges the stereotype that philosophy graduates face high unemployment?

• How do philosophy's universal skills (reasoning, communication, ethical judgment) translate into the workplace?

• Why do philosophy majors tend to perform strongly on graduate exams like the LSAT?

• What role does adaptability play in long-term career resilience?

Chapter 6 — From Classroom to Impact: A Philosophy Playbook for Real-World Results

• How can a Portfolio of Reason (PoR) help students demonstrate their skills to employers?

• Why is clear problem framing an essential skill for decision-making across disciplines?

• What does it mean to treat ethics as 'part of the design space' rather than an afterthought?

• How might cross-disciplinary collaboration benefit from philosophical methods of reasoning?

Chapter 7 — Philosophy as Meaning and Purpose

• Why can't Artificial Intelligence provide its own reasons for questions of 'why' (e.g., why live a good life)?

• How does philosophy help individuals and societies navigate rapid technological or cultural change?

• What is the difference between intelligence and wisdom, and why is this distinction important?

• How can philosophy help families and communities respond to tragedy or adversity with resilience?

Chapter 8 — Philosophy as Society's Compass

• What does it mean to describe philosophy as society's compass?

• How does philosophy guide science and technology toward humane ends?

• In what ways does philosophy provide a common language across cultural or political divides?

• Why is philosophical clarity especially vital during crises such as pandemics or wars?

Chapter 9 — Philosophy as Preparation for Life

• What practical tools from philosophy can help individuals make better decisions under uncertainty?

• How does philosophy foster resilience and principled character in daily life?

• Why is financial reasoning also a philosophical question, not just a numerical one?

• How does philosophy strengthen civic literacy and public reason in democratic societies?

Chapter 10 — Philosophy as Guidance for Parents and Counselors

For Parents

• Why do parents often worry about philosophy as a major, and how can these concerns be addressed?

• How might philosophy help bridge the generational gap between parents and children?

• What benefits can parents themselves gain from studying or exploring philosophy?

For Counselors

• How can counselors use philosophy to guide students toward resilience and purpose in their education?

About the Author

L. R. Caldwell is an independent philosopher and author whose work bridges metaphysics, science, and contemporary philosophy of mind. With nearly five decades devoted to studying and reflecting on the deepest questions of consciousness, reality, and human purpose, Caldwell has developed an original framework known as the Consciousness Structured Field Theory (CSFT). This body of work challenges narrow materialist assumptions while offering a constructive new perspective on the role of consciousness in shaping human experience and the natural world.

He is the author of the acclaimed trilogy *The IF Trilogy: A Unified Theory of God, Mind, and Matter*, which spans theology, philosophy, and science to present a coherent exploration of reality's foundations.

Each volume demonstrates Caldwell's ability to unify profound metaphysical inquiry with rigorous analysis, positioning philosophy not as an abstract pursuit but as a discipline with deep relevance for students, educators, and families alike. His subsequent book, *Consciousness: Beyond the Planck Boundary*, continues this trajectory, focusing on the relationship between consciousness and the quantum field, extending philosophical reflection into the cutting edges of science. His book, titled - "The Case for Philosophy in Higher Education: *A Guide for Building Purpose, Skills, and Resilience in College and Beyond"* details the importance of Philosophy as a basis' to higher learning and advancement in nearly every field of both study and employment.

In addition to his books, Caldwell has published over thirty papers on PhilPapers, the international archive of philosophical research. His papers span topics in philosophy of mind, neuroscience, consciousness studies, and quantum field theory.

By weaving together historical insights, contemporary science, and clear metaphysical reasoning, Caldwell's work contributes to ongoing dialogues in both academic and independent philosophy circles. His contributions are noted for their originality, clarity, and ability to engage enduring philosophical problems in ways that invite students and scholars into meaningful conversation.

While Caldwell has, at times, gone head-to-head with academia, this should never be seen as a dismissal of higher education. On the contrary, he maintains the highest regard for academia and its essential role in shaping lives and fostering intellectual growth.

His independent stance complements, rather than rejects, the traditions of scholarly research, allowing his work to serve as both a partner to faculty inquiry and an accessible guide for students and parents who recognize the importance of philosophy in education.

Caldwell's mission is to advance philosophy as a living discipline that equips individuals with purpose, resilience, and critical thinking skills. For faculty, his work offers new avenues for intellectual exploration; for parents, it highlights philosophy's power to nurture clarity, ethics, and direction in their children's lives.

Through books, articles, and public engagement, Caldwell continues to emphasize that philosophy is not an isolated or outdated pursuit but a foundation for education, character, and the human search for meaning.

www.ingramcontent.com/pod-product-compliance
Lightning Source LLC
Chambersburg PA
CBHW051432090426
42737CB00014B/2938